CA$H INJECTION PLANNER

for Entrepreneurs

A Fast-Action Guide for Bringing Cash Into Your Business In the Next 7 Days

MICHELLE KULP

ISBN: 978-1-7373222-6-9

TABLE OF CONTENTS

INTRODUCTION

Entrepreneurs love coming up with new ideas so much that it's safe to say they are *Idea Generating Machines*. The average entrepreneur probably comes up with 100 ideas before breakfast. I know I do.

However, like Guy Kawasaki so eloquently reminds us, "*Ideas are easy. Implementation is hard.*"

Many entrepreneurs aren't able to execute their ideas because they:

- Don't have the team to implement their ideas because they are wearing too many hats in their business.

- Spend too much time "researching" and not enough time executing.

- Underestimate entirely the time involved in executing the idea.

- Over-complicate their ideas.

- Find a new shiny object (new idea) to chase after when the going gets tough.

- Ask others what they "think" of the idea and let those answers drive their actions instead of asking people to pull out their credit cards.
- Have subconscious *money blocks* that cause them to do everything except "make money" or "make a profit."
- Focus on *busy work* like business plans, logos, graphics, and social media instead of doing the work to move the idea into the money-making stage.
- Have too many projects and can't seem to focus on just one.
- Don't know which program or product is their *Main Money Maker* (MMM–the one with the highest profit margin) and, therefore, don't focus on it.
- Are over-doing and under-outsourcing.
- Delay implementation too long after developing an idea.
- Fear the power, responsibility, and accountability that come with having a lot of money, so they self-sabotage.

I'm sure you can relate to some or maybe all of these reasons for getting stuck, not achieving your goals, and ultimately failing.

I can too.

I've been an entrepreneur running my online business since 2005. Before starting my online business, I had a 17-year career in the legal field as a paralegal, where I was told what to do, when to do it, and how to do it. I was a cog in the wheel of a well-oiled machine.

The "machine" had to generate tons of cash to keep operating, and the #1 responsibility for each lawyer was BILLABLE HOURS.

Here's the thing about business and entrepreneurship.

No one is going to tell you what to do.
No one is going to save you.
No one cares about your
business as much as you do.

The #1 reason businesses fail is a *lack of cash.*

Now if you were a lawyer, it would be ingrained into your brain that your #1 job is "billable hours." Unfortunately, entrepreneurs aren't trained in the same way.

Consider this book a reminder that your #1 priority in your business is to generate cash, and your #2 priority is to manage the cash flow so that you are *profitable* and don't run out of money in the future.

Most entrepreneurs have two BIG issues when it comes to money:

1. CASH FLOW
2. PROFIT

You NEED *cash* in your business, or you won't have a business. Also, you NEED to be *profitable* to keep your business going for years to come.

Abraham Maslow taught us the "Hierarchy of Needs:"

1. **Physiological** – Air, food, water, shelter, sleep, etc.

2. **Safety** – Security and safety in your environment, health, and finances.

3. **Belongingness** – Love, friendship, community, family, and intimacy.

4. **Esteem** – Confidence, self-worth, self-esteem, achievement, and respect.

5. **Self-Actualization** – Creativity, self-expression, etc.

According to Mike Michalowicz, author of many business books such as *Fix this Next* and *Profit First*, a business also has a hierarchy of needs.

Below is a diagram from Mike's blog:[1]

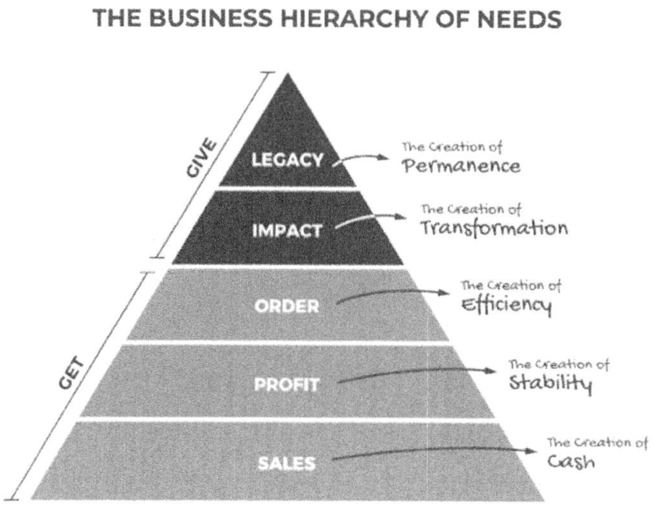

1. **Cash Creation/Sales** – Sales is the lifeblood of your business.

2. **Profit/Stability** – Even if you are great at sales, if you are not great at managing money, eventually, you will fail.

[1] https://mikemichalowicz.com/the-business-hierarchy-of-needs/

3. **Efficiency/System/Order**—Time is finite, so you must establish systems and be efficient to make the most of your time.

4. **Impact in the World** – Entrepreneurs are creators and want to be of service and impact others with their ideas.

5. **Leaving a Legacy** – What legacy will you leave behind when you are dead and gone?

You shouldn't work on these other areas of your business until you have mastered Cash Creation/Sales and Profit/Stability.

Cash & Profit are the foundation of a healthy business.

I created this *Cash Injection Planner* to help entrepreneurs become laser-focused on "Cash Flow & Profit." Once that is achieved, they can concentrate on other areas of their business and reduce the risk of having to close their doors due to cash flow issues.

It's easy to stay "busy" with fun things like designing websites and logos, finding cool images for your blog posts, doing Facebook lives, running ads, etc. Still, at the end of the day, you need to be a "Cash Creation Ninja" or a "Money Magician." Otherwise, you will find yourself broke, struggling, and in a constant state of panic.

In Mike Michalowicz's book, *Profit First: Transform Your Business from a Cash-Eating Monster to a Money-Making Machine*, he says that most business owners have the traditional accounting method backward, which is:

"Sales-Expenses = Profit"

Entrepreneurs typically run their businesses by selling as much as they can, paying the bills, and whatever they have left over is profit. The problem with doing business this way is that there is typically nothing left, and many entrepreneurs just keep paying the bills and putting anything extra back into the business.

Mike says, "This old profit formula creates monsters of businesses—cash-eating monsters. But we stay loyal to the formula, and things get worse."

Mike's answer: *TAKE YOUR PROFITS FIRST*

This *Cash Injection Planner* focuses on two main areas for your business:

1. Bringing in Cash with **HIGH-TICKET SALES** for your business in the next 7-30 days using the Minimum Viable Product (MVP) method.

2. Taking a profit before paying expenses so you can stay in business.

I want to help you exit the *feast-and-famine cycle* in which most entrepreneurs live. If you can generate cash and keep some profit month after month, you can become *PERMANENTLY PROFITABLE.*

Bringing ideas to life is miraculous, and being a creator is astounding. It's important to know the difference between making money and taking a profit because they are two very different things.

Money is the lifeblood of your business. You can bring in a million dollars per year and still not be "profitable" and stuck on the feast-and-famine hamster wheel.

Just turn on the inspiring television show "Shark Tank," and you'll see many examples of entrepreneurs who have 6- to 7-figure businesses with zero or negative profit.

So, if you're ready to:

1. Master your money.
2. Stay in business.
3. Have an impact.
4. Leave a legacy.

Let's get started...

CHAPTER 1

THE HOUSE IS ON FIRE!

Imagine this...

It's the middle of the night, and the smoke alarm goes off. The house is literally on fire. Smoke fills the rooms of your house quickly. Your baby is sleeping in the next room. You have two minutes to get out of the house, or you and your baby will die.

What do you do?

You move like a cheetah to get your baby and yourself out of the burning house in less than two minutes.

Nothing moves us into action quite like an ***EMERGENCY.***

But sometimes "emergencies" become Addictive Repetitive Patterns (ARPs).

If the same problem keeps showing up, you haven't addressed the root cause of the problem.

Many times subconscious patterns and habits are running our lives and businesses. We find ourselves in ***fight, flight, or freeze mode*** repeatedly. It typically looks like this:

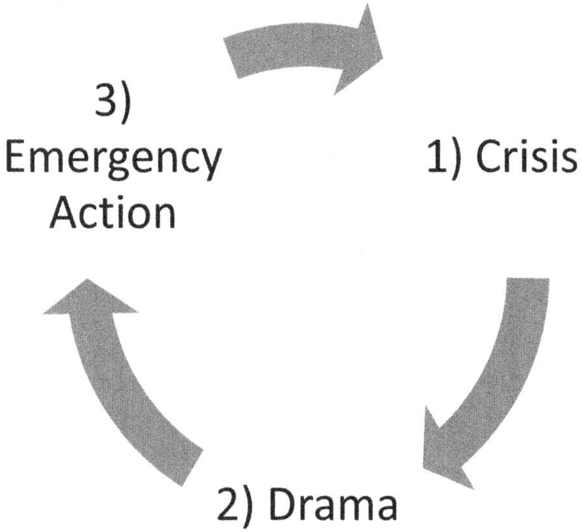

1. **Crisis** happens (subconscious patterns are running the show)
2. **Drama** ensues (we get a healthy dose of dopamine).
3. We jump into **emergency action** and save the day (more dopamine)!

Here is an example of what it might look like in action:

1. Cash flow emergency!
2. Can't pay the bills!
3. Employ ninja marketing tactics!
4. Sign up a new client or customer!
5. Pay the bills!
6. Celebrate by spending money you don't have!

Then… it happens again the next month, and the next, and the next.

Repeat, repeat, repeat.

If you have recurrent cash flow problems, you have to dig deep inside yourself and your business to unearth why this keeps happening.

Getting a new client and then paying the bills only to struggle again in a few weeks or months is no way to live or run a business. The new client you hustled to get that brings in cash during your cash-flow emergency is just a Band-Aid and won't prevent further problems.

So what is causing all of this?

Money Blocks — unconscious emotional patterns that are running the show.

7 COMMON MONEY BLOCKS

1. Past Experiences

Something in your past related to money (usually in childhood) made you believe that money was bad, evil, scary, forbidding, or dangerous.

For example, when I was a kid, I had a "Christmas Savings Account." I worked hard babysitting, selling lemonade in the neighborhood, doing household chores, making and selling crafts, and other odd jobs to put money into the account. One year, when I asked my parents to take the money out so I could purchase gifts, they said the money had been spent on bills because there was an *emergency* and they needed it.

I felt angry and devastated because I had worked hard for that money. As an adult, as soon as I would save money, an emergency would come up, and I had to use my savings. I was living paycheck-to-paycheck for years with zero in savings. I finally realized that I had an unconscious belief that it wasn't *safe* to save money because someone or something would always take it away.

Once I addressed this underlying issue, I was able to save $100K in 12 months and purchase a brand new construction dream home. I wrote a book about how I did this: ***Stop Living Paycheck to Paycheck.***

2. Religious Upbringing

Your religious training or upbringing taught you that money is the root of all evil and that it is a sin to love money. Because you want to be a "good" and "righteous" person, you subconsciously ignore money and probably have a love/hate relationship with it. If you have money, you are a terrible person, but you need money, which feels wrong too. It's a lose/lose situation.

3. Superiority Complex

You see yourself as an artist, creator, or inventor that is *ABOVE* petty things like dealing with money. You don't want to ruin your *art* by having to think about money. You're too good for that. So you ignore money until an emergency happens and you can't pay your bills. Then you have to step down from your High Artist Pedestal (HAP) and deal with the financial crisis like the rest of the world does. Many great artists were "broke artists" because they ignored everything related to money.

4. You Despise Sales

You subconsciously hate sales. You feel like the world of sales is full of charlatans, liars, and manipulators, so you don't want any part of it. This causes you to avoid making sales because your energy repels money coming to you. Unfortunately, you will not have a business if you don't sell your services or products. There are snake oil salesmen and women, but you don't have to be one of them.

4. Imposter Syndrome

You feel like a fraud, so you undercharge for your services. Have you ever heard the term "impostor syndrome"? Many people struggle with self-doubt, causing them to undervalue and undercharge for their services. Inside, you feel lucky that you can get paying clients, but you don't feel worthy of receiving money. Consequently, you never consider the cost of doing business to see if you are charging enough to make a profit. So, you continue to struggle and remain broke. You bury your head in the sand because you are subconsciously self-sabotaging yourself.

Because you have the impostor syndrome, you consistently under-charge and typically over-give because you are trying to PROVE YOUR WORTH and value to others. You're on a hamster wheel that you can't seem to get off.

5. Parents or Caregivers

Your parents or caregivers struggled all their lives to make ends meet, and it feels wrong to make more money than they made. Staying stuck at a certain income level makes you feel like you are still part of the family and tribe.

6. Living for Today

You are great at getting cash-paying clients, but then money burns a hole in your pocket, so you overspend – living the life of the rich and famous. When the bills come due, you're broke again. A *live-for-today* belief causes you to overspend because you believe you won't be here in the future or you'll deal with it later. Right now, it's about having fun!

7. Living on the Edge

You are addicted to drama, adrenaline, and dopamine; living on the edge is exciting and risky. You are essentially an adrenaline junkie! What better way to get a hit of adrenaline than having a monthly financial crisis to give you your fix? You may be trading one addiction for another.

* * * * *

These are just a few money blocks people have when it comes to money habits, patterns, and beliefs. The key is to examine these blocks and bring them out of the darkness and into the light. Most of our actions are driven by our subconscious minds.

Once you are aware of a pattern, you can address it. You may need support, therapy, or professional help, but at least you are willing to change your habits, so you can have prosperity and abundance in your life.

Like Dave Ramsey's successful *Financial Peace University*, the goal of this book is to help you have more *financial peace.* In order to do that, you must look deep into your money patterns and blocks.

List the top three Money Blocks described above that resonate with you.

1. ______________________________________

   ____

2. ______________________________________

   ____

3. ______________________________________

   ____

I wish I could snap my fingers and sprinkle magic fairy dust on you so that you feel worthy of having money, making money, and having financial peace. I can't do that, but you can.

Once you are aware of a pattern, it's much easier to break it because now you will begin seeing it in action, and you can catch yourself doing it and then take a pause.

For example, if one of your blocks is that "money burns a hole in your pocket" and you are "future-averse" (you spend now and live for today), becoming aware of this pattern and money block means that you can pause… and make a "RE-DECISION."

Ask yourself:

Do I want financial peace, or do I want to continue overspending and living in a constant financial crisis?

Instead of booking that trip to Vegas or the beach, plan an afternoon trip to a café or bookstore, work on how you will bring in cash, save some money, and apply it to your *Profit Plan.*

I promise that once you have $10K, $20K, or $50K+ in the bank, you will choose financial peace over short-term pleasure or fixes. If you have trouble sleeping at night, it might be because you have no financial safety net, and it's a scary way to live.

I recently read that 2/3 of Americans live paycheck-to-paycheck with no money in savings. You don't have to live that way; you have options if you treat your business like an asset.

Having money in savings for a rainy day isn't because you are superstitious or believe something bad will happen. The reality is that "rain happens" all the time in nature, and instead of wishing it didn't rain, take care of yourself and be prepared with a raincoat, umbrella, rain boots, and a hat so you're NOT soaking wet, cold, and shivering.

It's time to take care of yourself by protecting yourself through your financial well-being.

Write your top three money blocks on an index card and put it somewhere you will see them every morning. Start catching yourself when you are making decisions about your business based on old money habits and do something brand new:

PAUSE, then make a RE-DECISION

Pausing will help you stop the *automaticity* of the financial patterns running your life. Once you see it clearly, you can make a re-decision which is a new decision that brings you financial peace. You are bringing the patterns out of the darkness and into the light of your consciousness.

Keep affirming…

I can choose unconscious financial patterns or choose financial peace by making new choices.

Your goal is financial peace, and you are worth it. Don't let your past dictate your future. You are an adult, and you can make new choices now.

CHAPTER 2

DISCOVER YOUR DOMINANT MONEY ARCHETYPE

Many years ago, I came across a book by Deborah Price called "*Money Magic: Unleashing Your True Potential for Prosperity and Fulfillment,*" which helped me understand that we all have a money type. I went to her website and took this quiz:

https://moneycoachinginstitute.com/eight-money-types/

I discovered that my money archetype was ***The Magician,*** which Price describes as:

"The Magician is the ideal money type. Using a new and ever-changing set of dynamics both in the material world and in the world of the Spirit, Magicians know how to transform and manifest their own financial reality. At our best, when we are willing to claim our own power, we are all Magicians. The archetype that is active in your life now is the place you need to grow from. By understanding your own personal mythology and the history behind your current money type, you will become conscious of patterns and behavior that are preventing you from having the relationship with money you desire.

When you have reached the point of understanding and have become aware of all that you need to know at this point on your journey, you will be ready to transform your newly acquired consciousness into the reality of your life.

The Magician is fully awake and aware of herself and the world around her. The Magician is armed with the knowledge of the past, has made peace with her personal history, and understands that her source of power exists within in the ability to see and live the truth of who she is. Magicians know the source of power to manifest lies in their ability to tap into their Higher Power. With faith, love, and patience, the Magician simply waits in certainty with the knowledge that all our needs are met all the time.

Magicians embrace the inner life as the place of spiritual wealth and the outer life as the expression of enlightenment in the material world. They are infinitely connected."

As I looked back on my life, I realized I was always creating money out of thin air – even as a young child, some of my endeavors for making money include:

1. Finding lost dogs for cash rewards
2. Hosting lemonade stands and bake sales
3. Babysitting
4. Selling plants from our garden
5. Organizing neighborhood skits
6. Delivering newspapers with my dad

As I got older, I had other side hustles. Being a single parent with three kids and no child support, I was living paycheck-to-paycheck, and I had to create more money *magically*. Some of those endeavors included:

1. Selling *Christmas Around the World* (a network marketing company).
2. Being a part-time nanny
3. Selling Partylite Candles (a network marketing company)
4. Selling discounted energy (a network marketing company)
5. Delivering pizza kits for a nonprofit organization
6. Starting my own private process service business
7. Starting a cleaning company on the side
8. Starting a roommate matching service and running ads in the *Pennysaver* (pre-internet)

The point is that I am a *Money Magician,* and when times were tough, I knew how to create money out of thin air!

I encourage you to take the quiz to learn your money archetype:

https://moneycoachinginstitute.com/eight-money-types/

Which one are you?

Innocent	Burying your head in the sand when it comes to financial matters.
Victim	Blaming other people or circumstances for your problems.
Warrior	Setting out to conquer money and learning about how to do that through conflict.
Martyr	Spending so much time taking care of others that you neglect yourself. Trying to control others, living in high drama, and having unhealed wounds.
Fool	Always seeking a windfall of money and looking for financial shortcuts. The fool is a combination of Innocent and Warrior. Fools are easily distracted and money slips through their fingers.
Creator/ Artist	Are you on a spiritual or artistic path and it seems difficult to live in the material world, so you feel conflicted with money? On one hand, you love money because of the freedom it brings, but you have no desire to participate in the material world. You are stuck in a belief system that disempowers you to manifest money.

Tyrant	Tyrants hoard money and use it to control people, events, and circumstances. They want to win at all costs and are master manipulators. They are always going after more, more, more and are never satisfied.
Magician	Willing to claim your own power and manifest your own financial reality.

After taking the quiz, you will learn your primary archetype and sub-archetypes based on your answers. I retook the quiz while writing this book, and my results were:

1. Magician – 67%
2. Warrior – 34%
3. Creator/Artist – 25%
4. Fool – 17%
5. Tyrant – 9%
6. Martyr – 9%

The results of this quiz allow us to begin seeing our patterns and blocks so we can work on bringing them out of the darkness and into the light.

We always have work to do. There is no such thing as being perfect in any area.

If we look at my quiz results, we can see that the warrior energy in me probably comes from having been a paralegal for 17 years; I have a lot of "fight" energy which can be good and bad. As I've gotten older, I have learned to pick my battles and that my identity doesn't have to be a "fighter" of everything.

I also consider myself a creator/artist, and focusing on sales and marketing doesn't come naturally to me. I am a writer and an introvert who would rather sit alone in a quiet room and write. Learning about sales and marketing has taken years, and there was a great learning curve. A part of me doesn't want to deal with the material world.

I also have some "fool" energy, which means I am looking for a windfall. Who doesn't want a windfall, right?! It is true. I like to daydream about winning the lottery, and then I remember that money isn't going to fall out of the sky; I have to take action and work for it.

My lesser archetypes are the martyr and the tyrant, so I must be aware when I am in that energy. I have three adult children, and I can see how I've used money in the past to control certain outcomes with them.

Take the quiz and list your results below.

1. ______________________________

2. ______________________________

3. ______________________________

4. ______________________________

5. ______________________________

6. ______________________________

Now, transfer these results to a notecard and hang it somewhere that you will see it every day, and work on those energies that are not serving you.

If you scored high for the "innocent" archetype, then take your head out of the sand and start dealing with your money. Read books you would typically not read and increase your knowledge about finances.

If your scores for the "victim" energy were high, make a list of people you blame for your circumstances. For years, I blamed my ex-husband because he didn't pay any child support for our three children. Once I let go of that energy, I started channeling it into making more money. That's when I left my $50K per year paralegal job, moved into outside sales, and doubled my income while cutting my hours in half within 18 months. Victim energy was holding me back.

If you scored high on the creator/artist energy, think about how you avoid the material world and focus more on the spiritual, artistic, or ethereal world. The problem with this is that you have to pay bills because you live in the material world. I always fantasized that Prince Charming was coming to save me.

Guess what? Prince Charming never came. I had to become *Princess* Charming and take care of myself. I highly recommend reading "*Prince Charming Isn't Coming: How Women Get Smart About Money*" by Barbara Stanny.

You must have a healthy relationship with money, finances, and patterns to attract money. Otherwise, you will keep repeating the same unhealthy patterns.

Many of us learn patterns from our family of origin and then repeat, repeat, repeat.

My ex-husband is 60 years old and still living on the financial edge like he did when we were 18. Nothing has changed.

You have the power to alter your circumstances, and the main pathway to change is education, awareness, and, in many cases, having a good business coach or a therapist.

Now that you are becoming more aware of your patterns, I want to talk about a concept called *Minimum Viable Product (MVP).* When you need cash fast, you need an MVP, not a 100-page business plan, fancy website, or logo!

CHAPTER 3

MVP YOUR WAY TO CASH IN 30 DAYS

It was December 2019, and I had not written or published a book for a few years. I was feeling sad because writing is my passion, and I felt like I was always putting my clients' projects ahead of my own. Since 2013, I have offered 1:1 done-for-you services at BestSellingAuthorProgram.com.

After reading an article by ***Written Word Media***[2] that states the average author earning six figures in royalties has an average of 28 books published, I immediately thought:

"I'm going to write a book a month for a year and test this theory."

Then, I shared my intentions publicly for accountability and executed my idea.

---

[2] https://www.writtenwordmedia.com/author-income-how-to-make-a-living-from-your-writing/

Beginning in January 2020, I wrote, published, and launched a book a month for 12 consecutive months! At the end of those 12 months, I had generated $3,300 per month in passive income, which is more than some people get from their social security income!

In 2021, I repurposed those 12 books and created box sets and audiobooks. Eighteen months after writing that first book, I generated $4800+ a month in passive income from my books!

Once I was successful at this, I created my *Digital Retirement* online course to teach other professionals how to create their own retirement income!

All of this happened because I executed an idea quickly.

Yes, it took me a year to write those 12 books, but I wrote and published the first book within 30 days and kept repeating that "action" for over a year!

Because of my *fast action*, the passive income I earn pays more than half of my monthly expenses.

Turn ideas into action items quickly if you want to bring cash into your business fast.

Many clients in my done-for-you bestselling author program have told me they previously worked on their book for years—sometimes 5 or 10 years! I've discovered this is very common, which is why they seek my help since they couldn't get the book done on their own.

Writing a book a month and generating almost $5K a month in passive income taught me a lot of valuable lessons I want to share with you:

1. Don't let the possibility of failure make you afraid to try new things; it's about learning what works and what doesn't in the shortest amount of time.

2. Treat everything like an experiment, and don't get too attached to the results.

3. Iterate. Create something, put it out in the world, and then tweak it.

4. 80% of my income comes from three of my books. I wrote 12 books in 12 months, and I would have never known which ones would be the most successful if I had not written ALL. OF. THEM. Everything can't be a home run, but remember that you only need a few home runs to hit your goals.

5. Once you have a home run, go all in on that and create new products and services.

6. *Execute fast* when you have an idea—no more than 30 days from concept to execution.

Eric Ries, the author of *The Lean Startup*, introduced the term "Minimum Viable Product" and describes it as follows:

"The first step is to enter the build phase as quickly as possible with a minimum viable product (MVP). The MVP is that version of the product that enables a full turn of the Build-Measure-Learn loop with a minimum amount of effort and the least amount of development time."

He is basically saying that rather than spending months or years creating a product, service, or book, do only the smallest amount of work required to truly test it.

I didn't know it at the time, but that's what I did when I was writing a book a month. I wrote only "short books" that I could write, publish, and launch in 30 days. I would have failed if I had tried to write longer books.

Essentially, I was testing titles and topics, and the market told me what my audience liked by what they bought. This is the "Build-Measure-Learn loop" that Eric Ries was talking about.

To get a CASH INJECTION into your business fast, you must create an MVP that can get you paying clients in 30 days or less.

One caveat I want to make is that *writing books* is not a way to create cash flow quickly—definitely not in 30 days. After you write and publish your book, you must launch your book, run Amazon ads, and market it to your audience.

Writing a book a month is definitely a ***slower path to income*** and is like a snowball that grows over time. The first month after launching my first book, my monthly income was about $200, then $400 the next month, and $600 the next. After 12 months, the monthly royalty was $3300; in 18 months, it reached $4800. It ebbs and flows.

Writing a book a month is not a CASH INJECTION strategy for this book because it's the long game.

I shared this example to show you how I executed an idea quickly, knowing it was an experiment without expecting immediate results. Because I have high-ticket programs that generate multiple six figures in my business, I was able to do this.

Once I found my home run ideas, I acted quickly to create *Digital Retirement Academy,* an 8-week guided program, which first launched in December 2022. The initial 7-day launch generated $20,000+ in income! We'll talk more about this later in greater detail.

The purpose of this book is to help you bring in high-ticket CASH INJECTIONS that bring in $1000 to $20,000+ fast.

There's a time for the slow path to wealth and a time for the fast past to wealth. And this, my friend, is about the fast path to wealth because your business depends on it.

Before we discuss high-ticket sales, I want to talk about the difference between sexy ideas and solving problems…

CHAPTER 4

SEXY IDEAS VS. SOLVING A PROBLEM

In 2018, I had a client, Lisa, an engineer who left her job at IBM to help people get started in real estate investing. Her niche was teaching people to buy properties in working-class neighborhoods in the $30K - $50K range.

We struggled to come up with a "sexy idea" for the book title. While researching keywords that buyers searched for on Amazon to find books on real estate investing, I discovered the keywords:

Investing in Rental Properties for Beginners

Guess what?

We stopped trying to come up with a "sexy idea" for her book title and instead made the wise decision to use the "exact keywords" people were searching for on Amazon for her book title because those keywords solved a problem and were benefit-driven.

When you are trying to develop a product, program, or service to offer to get a "Cash Injection" into your business, focus on solving problems instead of just having a sexy, artsy, poetic, or clever idea.

If you find a *need* in the marketplace that *solves a problem*, you can generate cash fast.

My daughter, Christine, has a woman-owned residential painting company specializing in kitchen cabinet painting, which solves a huge problem in the market. People don't want to spend a ton of money remodeling their entire kitchen when they can just paint their kitchen cabinets and have an updated and remodeled look.

Christine has also found that many people think they can DIY their kitchen cabinets and then call her to fix the damage they created when trying to do it themselves. Since starting her business a few years ago, she's never run out of projects or business. She's on her way to a million-dollar business as we speak!

The fastest path to a Cash Injection is solving a problem people have and being able to collect the cash quickly.

Christine collects 1/3 of the money upfront, 1/3 at the start of the job, and the final 1/3 when the job is complete.

My done-for-you programs are structured similarly, so I have money coming in every month. I also receive royalties from my books and income from my coaching program/course *Digital Retirement*. I call this multiple streams of cash!

Now it's time to brainstorm what problems you can solve.

I don't know your experience – whether you have a brick-and-mortar business, a product business, or an online business – but the best way to make cash fast is by offering a service people want.

There's a saying, "Give a man a fish, feed him for a day. Teach a man to fish, feed him for a lifetime."

In my online business, when it comes to publishing and launching books, my business clients don't have time for me to *teach* them how to do it; they want me to do it for them. Those packages start at $10K and go up to $40K+.

Now it's time to brainstorm. List any done-for-you services or high-ticket coach programs that you can offer right now using your email list, social media, or a network that you know is in high demand:

1. ______________________________

2. ______________________________

3. ______________________________

4. ______________________________

5. ______________________________

6. ______________________________

7. ______________________________

8. ______________________________

If you need some ideas, here are a few resources to look at:

1. www.Fiverr.com
2. www.Upwork.com
3. https://www.PivotPlanet.com/browse

It's essential to use a skillset you already have. Do NOT come up with ideas for services if you have no experience providing those services.

Everyone wants to make passive income, but it's not as easy as it sounds, and it typically takes a long time to see results. Remember, my book-a-month experiment took me 12 months to create $3300 a month in passive income. When you need money now, long-term strategies won't help.

You need fast cash fast.

Offer something that you have done and been successful with in the past and that you have the current skillset to execute on.

Are there other profit paths than done-for-you services?

High-ticket coaching is very lucrative, but it must be in-demand, and you must have the background, experience, and skill set to offer it. Otherwise, prospects won't believe you are an expert.

If I needed cash fast, I would offer a done-for-you service first and do a high-ticket group coaching program next.

Done-For-You will bring in cash fast!

Whichever option you choose, you must be able to execute quickly and charge a premium for your services.

I built my entire multi-six-figure business doing done-for-you services.

Of course, there's another saying: "What got you here won't get you there."

I believe that to get to seven figures, I need to minimize my done-for-you services and do more group coaching because it's almost impossible to scale a done-for-you service unless you want to grow a huge company and manage employees, which is NOT what I desire at this time.

I've been doing done-for-you services since 2013, which has allowed me to have a multiple-six-figure business where I keep 70-80% of the profit; I operate this business with a handful of talented sub-contractors that I have vetted and worked with for years now. It's set up like a well-oiled machine.

Until you are doing six figures, I would recommend focusing on done-for-you services if you have a skill set that is in high-demand or high-ticket coaching in order to bring in cash fast.

Don't start with low-ticket courses. I tried that in 2005 and wasn't earning six figures until 2015—ten years later! I should have started with high-ticket offers and then created low-ticket offers once I had that working.

What's Your One Thing?

As I said in the Introduction, entrepreneurs are great at generating new ideas, but sometimes you have to pick ONE THING!

Entrepreneurs hate picking one thing!

In 2014, my online business was on the feast or famine rollercoaster that so many entrepreneurs experience. I took a leap of faith, and in September 2014, I hired my first high-ticket business coach, Jason Nyback. In 90 days, I tripled my income! I'll never forget what my coach said to me when he looked at my only website at the time – www.becomea6figurewoman.com. "What exactly do you do? You have ten offers on that website. Pick one, and take everything else down."

My coach was a paid advertising guru, a prolific copywriter, and an amazing business coach on every level. I'll admit, it was hard for me to pick "one thing," but I was paying him a lot of money, so I looked at all my offers, and I picked an online course I was selling at that time for $197 — "Bestselling Author program." He told me he would help me turn that $197 course into a $5K+ program, and within 90 days, I would be selling out of my high-ticket (done-for-you) program.

I've earned six figures every year since as a result of picking my "one thing." In the past few years, I've hit multiple six figures. And it all happened because my coach taught me to focus on ***one thing***.

All businesses grow and evolve, but if you're making a little money from having a lot of offers, I am going to encourage you to do the same thing my coach had me do:

PICK ONE THING

Sometimes entrepreneurs go crazy chasing shiny objects. We also seem to have amnesia, and we forget what actually worked in the past for us.

My daughter, Christine, who I mentioned earlier, had a hard time picking her "one thing" initially; on her website, she offered three services:

1. Residential painting
2. Murals
3. Kitchen Cabinet Painting

Quickly, she learned it was too hard to manage all three services, so she had to pick one lane and stay in it. She selected "kitchen cabinets" (which she is really great at), and her business is flourishing as a result.

Think back to some of your past offers that did well financially and list them below.

1. ______________________________
2. ______________________________
3. ______________________________
4. ______________________________
5. ______________________________
6. ______________________________
7. ______________________________
8. ______________________________
9. ______________________________
10. ______________________________
11. ______________________________
12. ______________________________

Next, narrow it down to your top three.

Finally, pick your top ONE!

My ONE THING IS...

Instead of reinventing the wheel, take a step back and see what has worked. It's easy to get off track trying to create new program after program, offer after offer.

I once had a client who had 20 different offers on her website; the logic was that she makes a little money from a lot of programs.

I get it; it's easy to believe you should have something that will appeal to everyone who visits your site

But remember this piece of advice my coach gave me:

A confused mind never buys.

Too many options will confuse your prospects, who will likely leave your site to find that ***one*** program to help them solve the one problem that brought them to your site in the first place.

Pick one thing and make it clear on your site that's what you do. Take down anything else that isn't generating thousands of dollars per month for you.

Once you are profitable, consistent, and generating loads of cash, you can add more offers; but for now, I want you to pick one thing.

In the next chapter, we will talk more about fast money vs. slow money…

CHAPTER 5

FAST MONEY VS. SLOW MONEY

In early 2021, I received a message from a woman whose business was teaching women how to start publishing companies.

Since she was already a bestselling author of several books and was teaching others how to do the same, I wondered what I had to offer that would help solve her problem.

We scheduled a call where I learned that she wanted to become a *USA Today* and/or *Wall Street Journal* best-selling author.

We connected right away, spoke for a long time, and a week later, I messaged her saying,

"Hello, you do multi-author books for clients and teach women how to start publishing companies, and I get books to the USA Today and/or the Wall Street Journal bestseller lists, maybe we should do a multi-author book together and launch it to those top-tier lists?"

Within a week, we selected a title for our book, designed the cover, put up a sales page, started a private Facebook group, sent emails to our respective lists, and posted on social media.

Within 30 days, two strangers came together and filled 30 spots in a multi-author book, which, by the way, generated over $250,000 in gross income.

This is the difference between fast money and slow money! We executed our idea very quickly without over-planning. As soon as our sales page was up, we started signing up contributors for the book project.

We didn't research the idea exhaustively, over-complicate things, or think about it too long. We just jumped in with both feet, and through "imperfect action," we learned what worked and what didn't.

The Younger Self Letters launched in June 2021, and I'm happy to report that it hit the *USA Today* bestsellers list.

Did we make mistakes?

Yes. Absolutely. All the way to the bank. LOL

A year later, I piggybacked off the success of that book and did another multi-author book, ALL IN, that hit both *Wall Street Journal* and *USA Today* bestsellers lists and generated an extra $100K+ in my business!

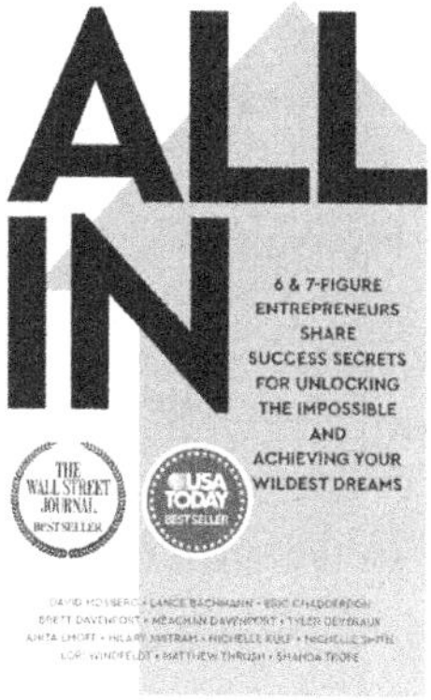

Follow these four steps to bring FAST CASH into your business:

Launch. Learn. Iterate. Repeat.

Using the systems created while launching "Younger Self Letters," I was able to take what I learned, make minor adjustments, and repeat the process.

Opportunity comes through hard work, commitment, and dedication.

I have one more story to share about a client who acted quickly on an idea and generated $23,000 from one webinar using someone else's audience!

From ZERO to $23,000 with one webinar

My client, Daniel, had a lot going on in his business and with his family, and he needed to generate cash fast.

I suggested that he host a webinar and create a course/ coaching program on the back end of one of his bestselling books in the financial field that I helped him launch earlier that year.

He quickly reached out to the top author and teacher in this space and offered him an affiliate commission for anyone who signed up for his new program.

In less than 30 days, he created the slides, set up the webinar, had the landing page ready to go, and with about 70 people on the live webinar, he signed up 23 people at $1000 each for a total of $23,000! After sending the replay out, ten more people signed up, generating an additional $10,000.

Desperation sometimes forces us to act quickly because we don't have much choice—it's either sink or swim.

Slow Money S-l-o-w-s You Down

Years ago, when I was working with my amazing business coach, Jason Nyback, I set up an automated webinar. Many of Jason's clients had their automated webinars set up within a month; however, it took me a lot longer. It was almost a year before my webinar was up and running…

That's called SLOW MONEY!

I wasted a lot of time and money by taking so long to create my automated webinar funnel. Eventually, once it was set up, it brought me so much business that I had to turn off the webinar along with the Facebook ads.

I'm sure underneath my *procrastination* were some of the money blocks I spoke about earlier.

A great book I want to recommend to anyone struggling with procrastination is *Procrastination: Why You Do It, What to Do About It NOW*, by Jane B. Burka, Ph.D. & Lenora M. Yuen, PhD

I love this book, and it has helped (and still helps) me overcome my procrastination tendencies in a BIG way by helping me understand why I procrastinate and giving me tools that work.

Before going any further, let's review a few tips for generating cash fast:

- Use a skillset you already have.
- Revisit past programs or offers that were successful and offer them again or do a new version of them with a twist.
- Choose services or programs that you can charge at least $1000 for.

- Don't make it complicated.
- Don't get bogged down doing research.
- Become aware of your money blocks and patterns so that you know when to pause and make re-decisions.
- Pick ONE thing.
- Solve a problem.
- Keep it simple.
- Remember, there is fast money and slow money. Which one do you choose?

Next, let's talk about which mistakes to avoid and how to act fast…

CHAPTER 6

AVOID THESE MISTAKES

In his book, the *7-Day Start-Up*, author Dan Norris says:

"If you have a conversation with a friend about your business idea this month, and next month, you are having the same conversation, you are a wantrepreneur."

A "***wantrepreneur***" is someone who talks about business ideas but never launches them.

Why would someone do that?

FEAR

We are all afraid that our launch will be unsuccessful, but the reality is… you don't learn until you launch.

Dan's story is pretty incredible…

> In 2007, he was one year into his first business. From 2007 to 2012, he made at most $40K per year in profit, and his actual wage dropped to below zero in

> 2013. He had no money and was two weeks away from giving up on his business and getting a job.
>
> His business generated money, but he needed more profit. Think of all that time he spent on this unprofitable business. He realized bringing in more revenue wouldn't solve the problem; his problem was a "profitability problem."

Have you ever watched the television show "Restaurant Impossible," where the host goes into failing restaurants to save them? The restaurant owner doesn't understand why they aren't successful, but it's usually because they don't know their food and operation costs. So although they might be selling food, they are losing money because their food and operations costs exceed their sales.

It isn't until they do a *deep dive* into all the costs for every item on the menu that they see where the problems are. Then, they can create profitable new menu items, and voila! The business is now profitable!

So what happens when we are backed into a corner and weeks away from going bankrupt...we have to launch fast.

That's what Dan Norris did. He sold his first company and started a new one using the following plan...

- *"Sexy ideas. I wanted to solve a problem and sell a service. Fast.*
- *My failure. I had failed a lot in 14 years, but I didn't have time to worry about my shortcomings.*
- *Permission. I used to ask for opinions on my ideas, but not this time.*
- *Assumptions. There was no time to make them or to test them. I had to launch.*
- *The small stuff. I didn't have months to agonize over a logo, business name, or design – I put the site up in one day.*
- *Pricing strategy. I set a price and would let my customers tell me whether it was worth it.*
- *The perfect payment gateway. Informly's payment gateway took six months to set up. This time, I used a PayPal button that I set up in 30 minutes."*

Do you see the difference here? He didn't have time to waste; he had to make this work fast.

He launched WP Live Ninja (now WP Curve), which is a WordPress support service that offers unlimited small WordPress jobs 24/7 for $69 a month.

A few days after launching the service, he had his first paying customer.

By the end of the first week, he had signed up ten paying customers.

Within 23 days, he was covering his expenses, and within a month, his business grew by 15% from word of mouth.

After 13 months, he had 475 customers and was making $33,000 in monthly recurring revenue (MRR).

He finally hit his profitability goal, which was to earn $100K annually. In fact, he exceeded that goal!

The interesting part of this story is that Dan didn't create a "high-ticket" program; he created a done-for-you service. Remember, people love done-for-you!

It's important to understand that not everyone wants to learn *how* to do something. Many people don't have the time or the interest, they just want it done.

Dan wasn't selling a program to teach prospects how to fix WordPress problems; he had a team of experts that would do it for them for a low monthly fee of $69. He had volume, and that's how he became profitable.

I can see how an entrepreneur could have spent months trying to launch this type of business, but Dan didn't have months to waste. He needed cash fast, or he would have to get a job.

Pain is a great motivator!

Now let's talk about another common problem with entrepreneurs… hustling.

CHAPTER 7

HUSTLERS VS. ANTI-HUSTLERS…

People often think they are hustling, but if what you're doing isn't making money, it's the wrong type of hustling: I call it *anti-hustling.*

Anti-hustling is what wanna-preneurs do. They do everything other than what needs to be done to generate cash.

I'm guilty of this as well. As I mentioned earlier, it took me a year to complete and launch my automated webinar after hiring my business coach. I made it harder than it should have been since I had no hard deadline to get it done (part of why I wasn't pressed is because I had a cushy outside sales job that paid my bills). I wasn't in enough pain.

I did my PowerPoint slides over and over, trying to make them perfect, and guess what? They never were perfect. One of the biggest challenges that my coach pointed out was that I was trying to teach everything I knew about publishing and becoming a bestselling author in a 45-minute webinar instead of doing a high-level overview of what I knew and showing the results my clients and I were having, including a call to action, and booking calls.

That was it. I was confusing the two, which is why it took me a year to get it going.

Next, I had to learn all about Facebook ads. It was hard, but I made it even more complicated by trying to figure out everything before getting started.

The name of the game with any paid advertising is to gather data, see what works and doesn't work, and scale once you have a winning ad.

I discovered that it wasn't about what I liked or thought people would like to see in the ads; it was about what enticed someone to click and then book a call with me. In other words, the data would tell us what people liked or didn't like.

Once my automated webinar and Facebook ads were up and running, I had a sustainable business. My coach used to say, "If you don't have paid ads, you don't have a business."

Having an automated webinar and paid ads provided me with a consistent stream of leads for my high-ticket program.

In 2017, I discontinued my ads because I was so busy with repeat clients and referrals that I didn't need more clients.

Remember, at the time, I only offered done-for-you, and you can't typically scale done-for-you. Now I have done-for-you, done-with-you, and do-it-yourself.

If you need money fast, paid ads can generate new leads, but you obviously must have the money to spend on ads.

At the time, I started by spending $10 per day on Facebook ads and gradually increased it to $700-$1000 per month. My programs started at $5K, so signing up one client would pay for the Facebook ad spend.

Hustling is doing things that generate cash and knowing the profitability of your business.

Anti-hustling is taking a year to create webinar slides and procrastinating about everything that makes money in your business.

A true hustler focuses on only three things:

1. Getting customers
2. Making a profit
3. Rinse and Repeat

And don't take a year (like me) to get customers by distracting yourself or trying to make everything perfect; do what Mark Zuckerberg once advised:

"Move fast and break things."

That's the name of the game. Move fast, and figure out what works and, more importantly, what doesn't.

A great movie that will inspire you is "Bezos: The Beginning." It was far from perfect, but he kept moving forward. And by the way, Jeff Bezos changed the name of the company three times until he finally landed on the name: "Amazon."

A lot of people get hung up on naming their product or deciding what to include in it.

Unfortunately, you don't get to decide—the market does.

The only way to know if you have a valid product or name is to experiment by doing the following:

1. Create a landing page and pre-sell it.
2. Get a minimum of $10K in pre-sale of your product.
3. Obtain a conversion rate is 30% or higher to know that you have a great product.

NOTE: Someone opting into your email list or signing up for a free strategy session or a waiting list does NOT indicate purchase intent.

There is a huge difference between someone sharing their email address and someone giving you their credit card to pay you for a product or service.

Why?

Because it's easy for a prospect to give you an email address, and it's hard for them to pull out a credit card and give you money.

So asking people what they think of an idea is not validation, especially if you are not asking your ideal client.

The only way to know for certain is to launch the idea or product and see if anyone pulls out their credit card.

However, be aware that you could lose money on that product if you don't know how much of your time and effort will be required or if the expenses are too high.

I often tell clients to double the price of what they think they should charge. The first time you make an offer (your

BETA or your Founders offer), you can price it lower than you normally would. But for our purpose, your minimum price will be $1,000.

In the past, I made a huge mistake by undercharging for my services. My coach told me to charge $5K when I first started working with him; I didn't believe people would pay that much, so I under-charged and sold my first done-for-you service for only $3000.

A funny thing happened. Practically every lead I had, I sold them into the program. It was easy peasy. But because it was a done-for-you service, I could only deliver that program to a few clients a month. It was too labor-intensive on the back end. I was probably losing money if you looked at how much time I had to spend delivering the goods.

The following month, I raised the price to $4K and sold out with four clients.

Finally, I raised the price to $5K and sold out again.

Now I charge $10K-$40K for my done-for-you services because it is very labor-intensive for my team and me.

$5K could be a good price point for a done-WITH-you program that involves you coaching someone on what to do or with a few done-for-you elements; 100% done FOR you is a whole other story.

As an example, my 12-week bestselling author Done-For-You program includes:

- Calls with me on book creation and strategy
- Editing of the book
- Formatting for eBook and print editions
- Cover design
- Publishing
- ISBN registration
- Coaching on back-end sales and building an email list
- #1 bestseller 2-day book launch
- Amazon ads expert to continue book sales
- Podcast interviews

I also have a program where we ghostwrite the book for clients that starts at $40K.

My point is that selling something doesn't mean you have a profitable business. If you can't take on ten clients at that price point, you should raise the price.

I'm going to repeat this again…

When you need money fast, the best way to generate cash is to offer a done-for-you service.

I did this years ago when I needed cash fast and started offering web design. I took a six-week course on WordPress web design, and within a few months, I had a very lucrative business. It's important to note that I have copywriting skills that enabled me to charge thousands of dollars for my services. I combined web design and copywriting and offered an all-inclusive done-for-you package.

I see a lot of website development companies putting up pretty websites with bad content that don't generate any money.

I'd rather have an ugly website with good copy that generates cash.

Spend your time on cash-generating ideas, not making things pretty.

Rather than investing in a bad website, invest in learning copywriting because it is a skill that can make you money over and over and over.

I've had clients invest $10K on a bad website, but because of poor copywriting, it doesn't generate money for them.

So those are a few pitfalls you should be aware of when testing your idea.

Just because something sells once doesn't make it a sustainable or profitable business. You must know your numbers and how much work is required on the backend.

Now let's look at a case study for generating fast cash…

CHAPTER 8

CASE STUDY: 7 DAYS TO $20K

After "thinking" about creating my Digital Retirement Academy for a year, I finally *tricked* myself into launching the brand new program in December 2022.

"Thinking" about things or doing endless "research" can make it seem like we are "taking action" toward our goals when in reality, we are just on a hamster wheel going nowhere!

The following image represents me spending a year on the hamster wheel... researching course platforms, comparing shopping carts, taking surveys on my course title, second-guessing the price I should charge, rewriting the curriculum, talking about it ad nauseum to others, yada yada yada!

So, how did I trick myself into launching this program and generating $20K+ in 7 days?

Funny you should ask…

Something that always works well for me is knowing that when I invest money in a coach or a done-for-you service, I will show up and do the work. I hate to waste money!

A year earlier, I was approached by a copywriter who worked with other authors helping them launch new programs. He offered to work with me for a fee. I wasn't ready for him just yet, but I finally reached out to him and hired him months later. It was a $3000 investment plus

30% of sales (similar to an affiliate commission) up to $100K on the launch.

The beauty of it was that he would write the sales page and the emails (16 total) and provide a launch plan for scheduling the emails and shopping cart.

Once I paid him the $3000, my team and I got to work.

You might be thinking, "Michelle, I don't have that kind of money."

First, that's probably not true. If your child or relative needed emergency surgery to save their life, you could come up with $3000.

I didn't have an extra $3000 lying around at that time either because I had recently paid a huge tax bill, bought a house, and had some other unexpected expenses. So I put the $3000 on a credit card and got to work.

As soon as I had to do the "work," I admit that I had a few moments of "Why did I do this? Now I have to do all this work!" But once I started, I actually got very excited, and everything started flowing.

I mistakenly thought that once we had the sales page up, people could sign up anytime, and we would allow people to register for a month or so, but the copywriter/launch expert said to leave the shopping cart open for 7 days ONLY.

I honestly thought it wouldn't work, but luckily I was wrong.

Scarcity and urgency influenced people to sign up for the program. The offer had a clear open date, and some emails were sent in advance of the opening to build anticipation for the program. There was also a clear close date, which was included on the shopping cart.

Here's a summary of the income that was generated during those seven days (after Christmas and during the New Year's holiday):

Day 1	$7000
Day 2	$997
Day 3	$1994
Day 4	$8,973
Day 5 (Holiday)	$0
Day 6	$997
Day 7	$997
Total Sales	$20,958

I feel that we had a great launch for the first offering of my new program, ***Digital Retirement Academy.*** I'm good with $20K! Of course, I would have loved a $100K launch, but honestly, I have 17 people in the first cohort, and it's the right amount of people to be able to help them write their first book and launch it to the bestsellers list.

Here's the difference between having a strategy vs. NOT having a strategy:

Two years earlier, I created a program called *28 Books to $100K,* which was a DIY program that I sold for $297; I didn't have a launch strategy like I did with *Digital Retirement Academy.*

I nonchalantly mentioned it on social media, put a link on my website, and left it open all year round. In one year, I made $20K.

This is a good example of *slow money vs. fast money* and learning what works and what doesn't.

In seven days, I made $20K vs. making $20K in 365 days. Which would you rather have?

Creating a program or service and putting up a sales page isn't a great strategy. I did make money on that program over time, but I could have made a lot more, probably at least $100K, if I had done a proper launch with a shopping cart that was only open for a limited time.

Now I can make *Digital Retirement Academy*, an 8-week guided course, into an evergreen program and sell it 24/7.

There are different schools of thought on doing a live launch vs. evergreen, so you have to decide for yourself.

I chose to do the live launch method for the first offer and close the cart to ensure everyone who joined would be at the same point in the curriculum during the 8-week program.

Another secret I want to share with you is something I call:

SELL THEN TELL

(that's the title of my next book, by the way)...

I didn't create any content for *Digital Retirement Academy* until after I sold $20K. I did, however, have the curriculum outlined because I used it on my sales page so anyone who signed up would know what they would learn during the course.

First, I created a pre-planning module so that new students could log in and start watching videos. The official start date for the live Zoom coaching calls was two weeks after the launch.

I then created the modules and uploaded them weekly into SamCart, which is the shopping cart I chose to use and where I host my online videos and course.

I've used several different programs since 2005, and I found SamCart to be user-friendly and easy to set up. I signed up for their "Growth" program on a free trial and made $20K before paying them a dime. I highly recommend them for your sales page, shopping cart system, and course hosting!

So, "*Sell then Tell*" is about not getting hung up on creating all the content before launching. It's about first making money and then creating the content.

There is actually a BIG problem when you create content first and then try to sell it. The problem is that you don't know whether you have a winning idea until people actually pull out their credit cards. So you're better off creating a sales page, doing a launch, and seeing if your offer sells ***before*** you create the content.

I've heard many stories over the years from entrepreneurs who say they spent months and sometimes years creating and launching a program with either no sales or only a few. Some entrepreneurs just refunded the money and never ran the program. What a waste of time and money.

Always sell then tell.

Also, just because you launch a program and it doesn't sell, it doesn't mean you don't have a winning idea. Other reasons could be:

- You have a bad sales page that isn't conveying the offer properly.
- You have a bad shopping cart program and are losing sales there.
- You have a bad title for your program, and people are confused.

Sometimes, you have to do more testing and change things as you go along.

When I was running Facebook ads, we tested three items before we had a "winning ad:"

1. Headline
2. Image
3. Call to Action

We ran three ads with three different headlines for about 3-7 days; the data told us the best headline by the number of clicks. Once we had our winning headline, we would run the winning headline with three different images for 3-7 days; the data would once again tell us which image was best based on clicks. With our winning headline and image, we would test three different calls to action; the data would give us the answer based on clicks. That's how we created winning ads!

The same is true for your offer, whether it's a service, online course, or done-for-you program.

Don't write off a bad launch as not fixable. You have to test different parts of your offer (sales page, program title, pricing, people you are offering it to, etc.).

Now that you've learned what to do and what not to do, let's make your plan for launching your new offer and bringing some fast cash into your business...

CHAPTER 9

THE 7-DAY PRE-LAUNCH STRATEGY

Let's look at a 7-day Pre-launch strategy according to Dan Norris:

Day 1

Generate a good idea. Learn to tell the difference between a bad idea and a good idea. Good ideas solve problems that people are looking to solve, and there are solutions in the marketplace to prove your idea is already making money. You just have to put your unique spin on it.

Day 2

You must have a tangible product to launch at the end of seven days, which will be your MVP (minimum viable product). Sell then tell. If you are launching an online course, concentrate on creating the sales page and perhaps one or two modules, and then you can drip the rest of the modules over the term of the course.

Day 3

Determine a business or product name. Don't overthink this. I got stuck on this step, but I took a poll in one of my Facebook groups with readers of my books, and they voted on *Digital Retirement Academy*, making the decision for me. Pick a "good enough" name.

Day 4

You need a landing page or a website that you can build in one day (Samcart is easy to use and doesn't require you to have a website so that you can get it up in one day).

Day 5

Utilize free methods to get your idea in front of people to decide whether to continue (I used my email list of 5000+ and my social media).

Day 6

Establish a benchmark to measure the program's success. *To move forward with teaching the program, I wanted at least 10 people enrolled ($10K), and we doubled that number!*

Day 7

Launch (just do it!)

Now it's time to plan your launch to bring some cash into your business.

What are you going to sell? That's the BIG question, right?

Listed below are 40 ideas to get some fast cash into your business:

1. Digital Online Course (6, 8, or 10 weeks)
2. Mini Online Course (4 weeks or less)
3. Weekend Masterclass
4. Live Course (not pre-recorded)
5. Joint-Venture online course taught with another instructor
6. Membership site
7. 1:1 Coaching
8. Group Coaching
9. Done-With-You Coaching
10. Done-For-You Coaching
11. Do-It-Yourself

12. Paid Webinar

13. Watch Me Do It Live

14. Watch With Me Recorded

15. Power Hour

16. Live Workshop or Seminar

17. High Ticket Coaching or Consulting

18. Mastermind Group

19. VIP Virtual Half Day

20. VIP Virtual Full Day

21. Certification Program

22. Licensing Intellectual Property

23. Business in a Box

24. Done-For-You Service

25. Done-With-You Service

26. Livestreaming Event

27. Sell Affiliate Products

28. Sell Technical Services such as Virtual Services, SEO services, website design, etc.
29. Online Consulting
30. Translation Services
31. Sell Skills on Fiverr
32. Tech Support services
33. Developing Online Courses for Others (Curriculum or tech)
34. Bookkeeping Services
35. Accounting Services
36. Relationship Advice
37. Editing and Proofreading Services
38. Social Media Management Services
39. Personal Training Services
40. Nutrition Plans

Pick one that matches your existing skillset and is an in-demand problem people want solved.

My offer is:

____

I am going to charge at least $1000 for this program ($1K to $5k+). My price for this program is:

____

(Remember, if you offer something like virtual assistant services, which could range from $20 an hour to $50+ an hour, create a package with a minimum number of hours to reach $1000/month). Don't undercharge!

List the ten steps you need to take to launch this offer (Minimum Viable Product). For example, sales page, hiring a copywriter, launch expert, tech person, virtual assistant, software, etc.

1. ____________________________________
2. ____________________________________
3. ____________________________________
4. ____________________________________
5. ____________________________________
6. ____________________________________

7. ______________________________

8. ______________________________

9. ______________________________

10. ______________________________

Don't try to do everything yourself. Get help and hire someone who is invested in your success and is on board with fast cash vs. slow cash.

I will hire this person(s) to help me…

____

____

____

____

My definition of success for this program will be (determine the number of enrollments needed to meet your goals). You decide…

____

____

____

____

I'm going to launch my program on this date (no longer than 30 days from today)...

____

What are the top three obstacles preventing me from reaching my goal?

1. ____

2. ____

3. ____

If you can foresee what will block you, you will have a better chance of success. My #1 obstacle is *paralysis by analysis*, so I hired a copywriter/launch expert because I knew that on my own, I would continue doing endless research and have no real or hard deadlines.

Once you have a successful launch, you can build on it by adding VIP days, masterminds, or other high-ticket offers.

For my *Digital Retirement Academy* launch, the minimum package was $997. I had one upsell for $2497 for three 1:1 coaching calls with me. Two people added the upsell, generating an additional $5000.

Think of one "upsell" you can include with your original offer that can really increase your sales numbers...

I've learned from using Samcart that profits increase exponentially with upsells, and you are leaving money on the table if you don't offer any.

For *Digital Retirement Academy*, I also offered payment options, so instead of one $997 payment, they could choose to make three payments of $367, increasing the price from $997 to $1100 (more profits). A few students signed up for the payment plan.

Payment plans enable more people to sign up for a course, especially if it is being taught over several weeks and is higher priced.

Years ago, after leaving my 17-year career in the legal field, I worked in outside sales selling hot tubs. I went from law to hot tubs!

I sold a high-ticket product, in-home, in a 100% commission job, on a one-call close. It was a little stressful, to say the least. I realized that the high price of the hot tub or swim spa sometimes scared potential buyers, but if I offered them a credit option with payments, the $10,000 hot tub might only be $250 per month, and they could have their dream hot tub *now* (instant gratification). It made selling a lot easier.

* * * * *

Congratulations! You have a ***Cash Injection Plan***. It's time to execute. To increase your odds of executing:

- Hire people to help you.
- Have an accountability partner.
- Set hard deadlines.
- Tell your family, friends, and followers what you are doing (so if you don't do it, you'll look bad).

I'm sharing what worked for me and what didn't work.

Of course, we all dream of having a $100K launch of our offer, but $10K or $20K can be life-changing and get you off the financial cliff and on to the next step in your business.

Now that I have created and launched *Digital Retirement Academy* and have "proof of concept," I can build on that. I plan on offering that program every two months (six times per year). If I do $20K+ for each launch, that is $120K extra in my bank account! Also, I can create content once and make money over and over, which is my favorite business model!

How would an extra $20K be for your business right now?

Get busy with your cash injection plan now and give yourself a 30-day deadline!

CHAPTER 10

PROTECTING THE PROFITS

As an entrepreneur, solopreneur, and/or CEO, you have three main jobs:

1. Making money.
2. Investing in skills that will make you even more money.
3. Re-investing your profits to grow your business assets.

Unfortunately, entrepreneurs struggle to protect their business profits (I've struggled with it, too).

3 Warning Signs That Your Business Is In Trouble:

1. **You have gone 3-12+ months without making any money in your business** (sometimes, we are so busy with "life" emergencies that we put our business on hold to deal with them). I can assure you that Jeff Bezos didn't put Amazon on hold when he was going through his divorce. You can't pause your business, or you won't have a business.

2. **You have no idea how much money you make each month (or year-to-date), and you don't know your business expenses.** To succeed in business, you must take your head out of the sand and know your numbers. Many entrepreneurs showcased on the hit television show "Shark Tank," don't get a deal because they don't know their numbers. When I was in outside sales for ten years, I discovered that the most successful salespeople always knew their numbers (closing rate, sit rate, cancellation rate, average monthly sales, etc.).
3. **You are waiting for "others" to teach you how to make money.** Even if you hire an expert or a coach to help you, you still have to bring in money. You can't pause your #1 job, making money, or you won't have a business.

This book is a reminder to myself and to you that we have to wake up and treat our businesses like a professional and not like a hobby. We don't have the luxury of burying our heads in the sand when it comes to making money.

Tips and tricks to *protecting your profits* and staying financially healthy:

- You must always be making money.
- Always know your numbers each month.

- If you are investing in learning a new skill (which is great), don't let the new learning trump making money.

- You must still bring in money if you decide to change your offer or niche.

- *Don't go broke going elephant hunting.* My coach, Jason Nyback, taught me this when I wanted to shut down the part of my business that was bringing in money to chase elephants (higher-ticket clients). We must keep proven income streams coming in while we launch and grow new offers.

- Don't fire all of your clients because you have a new offer or business model. I've had clients do this in the past. My advice is don't give up existing cash flow while you are chasing something new that isn't bringing in money consistently.

- Always have a "Protect Your Profits" mindset. Your self-concept is that you are the "main money maker" of your business.

- Don't overspend on your personal or business expenses.

- Understand the difference between personal profits and business profits. Your business profits fund your personal profits.
- Don't fund your personal profits and give what's left over to the business. It needs to be the other way around.
- Commit to a business profit number and stick to it.
- Business profits must always be top of mind.
- If your business is broke, you may have to cut back on your lifestyle. Reduce your personal expenses.
- Always make sure your living expenses are below your personal expenses.
- Your business must be cash-flow positive, and you must have money in the bank. Three to twelve months of expenses is a good rule of thumb.
- Pay yourself, but ensure you have enough business profits to do so.
- If your business is struggling, create a "Hell Yeah" offer that people can't refuse. Think $10K to $50K+

- Make decisions from the future you vs. where you are now. For example, if you want a 7-figure business, make decisions from that future place rather than the 5- or 6-figure place you are at now.

- Don't take a personal or spiritual sabbatical and pause your profits. Businesses don't take breaks.

- You can't take a break when things get hard or the storms of life come. You must stay on track to protect your profits.

- Distinguish and separate your personal growth goals and your business growth goals.

- Business growth funds personal growth, not the other way around.

- Invest in your selling skills and your brain, but don't pause your business or go broke while you do so.

- No one else in your business is responsible for making money. This is your #1 responsibility.

- You will need three things to scale:
    1. Business mindset coaching
    2. Marketing
    3. Help (outsourcing)

- Don't pay yourself first at the expense of your business. Always protect the business and make changes in your lifestyle first to cut down your costs.

- Know your bottom line profit number each month and do what's needed to reach that goal.

- Act like you have employees to pay, even if you don't.

- Show up MORE than you did when you had a "job," not less. Don't have an employee mindset thinking someone else is responsible for making money.

I hope this book helps you as much as it has helped me while writing it.

I realize my biggest mistake was my mindset around business and treating it more like a hobby. Sometimes we start with a side hustle and keep our full-time job, but when you take the leap and go all in on your business, it's also essential to upgrade your mindset.

After all, you are the CEO of your business.

Your #1 responsibility and job is to make money and protect the profits at all costs. Go forth and make money!

Congratulations on all of your success!

Michelle Kulp

Notes

Notes

Notes

Notes

Notes

Made in the USA
Monee, IL
04 November 2026

67388650R10066